Cambridge Plain Texts

BYRON

THE VISION OF JUDGMENT

T0346091

BYRON

THE VISION OF JUDGMENT

CAMBRIDGE
AT THE UNIVERSITY PRESS
1926

CAMBRIDGE UNIVERSITY PRESS
Cambridge, New York, Melbourne, Madrid, Cape Town,
Singapore, São Paulo, Delhi, Mexico City

Cambridge University Press
The Edinburgh Building, Cambridge CB2 8RU, UK

Published in the United States of America by Cambridge University Press, New York

www.cambridge.org
Information on this title: www.cambridge.org/9781107626485

First published 1926
Re-issued 2013

A catalogue record for this publication is available from the British Library

ISBN 978-1-107-62648-5 Paperback

INTRODUCTORY NOTE

BIOGRAPHY. Byron's work cannot be properly understood without some knowledge of the circumstances of his life. His mother's ancestors, the Gordons, had intertwined their fortunes with those of the Stuart house, and given vent to their tempestuous natures in many daring enterprises. Two of his father's immediate forbears won notoriety; one, "Foul-mouthed Jack," as the most efficient swearer in the Navy, and the other for throwing through the window of his coach those who disagreed with his emphatic opinions. It is little wonder that their descendant by his life and his literature fluttered the dovecotes of English propriety. Byron's father, having spent all his wife's money, quarrelled with her continually, which caused their son little regret: "as she was as much a vixen as he a rogue," and neither the death of his father when he was a child, nor of his mother in his early manhood, gave him any grief.

After spending his early years in Aberdeen, he went to Harrow—one of the few objects of his genuine affection—and thence to Trinity College, Cambridge, where he diverted the neighbourhood, and demonstrated his zest for the limelight by keeping a bear. The customary Grand Tour had in his case to be varied owing to the Napoleonic wars, and he spent most of it in Spain and Greece, whence sprang his enthusiasm for the latter nation. He returned to England, and for a time was the darling of society, but he soon wearied of managing his Newstead estate with insufficient means

and of making occasional speeches in the House of
Lords. Moreover, he had by this time grown tired of
the prim and indifferent wife he had married two years
before, and it needed only the obloquy which descended
on him as a result of their divorce, to send him out of
England never to return to the country where his
irritable vanity was constantly outraged. For the next
five years he enjoyed himself on the continent, meeting
the Shelleys on the Rhine and in Italy. Most of
his poetic work belongs to this period, as well as
his connection with *The Liberal* which brought credit
neither to him nor to his co-editor Leigh Hunt.
Undoubtedly, his voluntary exile enabled him to adopt
a pose of personal isolation, and to fill his writings with
a fanfaronade of self-advertisement, while he criticised
the world with scornful mockery, and excited Europe
by his life of adventure, fittingly ended by the dramatic
heroism of his early death in the cause of Greek in-
dependence at Missolonghi in 1824, his age being
thirty-six.

QUARREL WITH SOUTHEY. The detailed history of
Byron's quarrel with Southey can be read in Lord
Ernle's edition of Byron's letters, from which it appears
that Byron was largely in the wrong, but the basic
cause of the feud was incompatibility of temperament.
Southey was narrow-minded and imbued with many
solemn and dangerous hypocrisies which led him to
call *Don Juan* "a lascivious book," but to hasten to the
defence of George IV in his divorce case. Byron was
bold and passionate, impatient of Southey's lack of
insight and "damnable complacency" and almost
gloated in focussing some of his contempt on a Poet
Laureate so void of his own desperate sincerity and

love of liberty. Thus it came about that *The Vision of Judgment* was issued anonymously in 1822 as a malicious and deliberate parody of Southey's eulogy on the death of George III.

OUTLINE. The scene is laid at the gate of heaven, when the angels are summoned from their respective tasks by the arrival of George III, brought thither that his everlasting doom may be determined; Saint Michael represents the powers of Goodness, while Satan comes to claim another King who had "paved hell with good intentions." After some argument, witnesses are called, and a multitude assembles, from amongst whom Wilkes and Junius become spokesmen.

While admitting his colourless domestic virtues, "chiefly constancy to a bad, ugly woman," it is pointed out that the King had always been the foe of liberty, though sometimes but "an old, blind, mad, helpless, weak, poor worm," the mere tool of his ministers, Pitt, Bute and Grafton.

His reign had seen the loss of America, the horrors of "the Gallic era," the execution of Louis XVIII, and finally the futile efforts for Catholic Emancipation. All these, however, Byron merely mentions—even the notorious Wilkes is only allowed a brief appearance to vote for George's "habeas corpus" into heaven, while the elusive Junius aroused only curiosity before he "melted into celestial smoke." The satirist has more palpable hits than these in his account of Fox's lard being used to baste William Pitt, and in his suggestion that the tumult of witnesses was comparable only to that in Parliament when Castlereagh spoke. There is, in Satan, a fine indifference to the King's fate, the matter being to him a mere case of "quit-rent," and the issue is in the balance, until Byron reaches his climax in the entrance of Southey, a heavy burden for Asmodeus, as though some of his books were hung round his neck.

The vast concourse of spirits, amazed at seeing one present who was not yet dead, provide Southey with an unusual audience, but before he can speak he is greeted by comments which give scope to Byron's most brutal bludgeonings. He is made to confess that he is one "who had turned his coat and would have turned his skin," since his is "a pen of all work" which has championed regicide and republicanism, warfare and pacifism, blank verse and blanker prose alternately. His halting hexameters cause anguish even in the precincts of heaven, his offer to "save the Deity worlds of trouble," by deciding the case is rejected; Satan refuses to allow his own biography to be a sequel to Southey's *Life of Wesley*, and amid the howling flight of his listeners, he is felled to the earth by Saint Peter, there to rejoin his wife at tea, while George III, having slipped unobtrusively into heaven, begins practising the hundredth psalm.

STYLE. The poem is shocking yet exhilarating, and prudence and morality must be set on one side in criticising it; it is a *tour de force* written exultingly, and untrammelled by any carefully developed scheme or detailed historical background, yet some of the character-drawing is subtle and majestic. Satan's hauteur is compared with that of an old Castilian noble, while his mind is full of unfathomable thoughts, and he is given a worthy opponent in Saint Michael, "a beautiful and mighty Thing of Light," who faces him with dignity and justice, and yet with some sense of immortal regret that destiny has ordained them to perpetual enmity. There is, moreover, a suggestion of the more devout side of Byron's own nature in his refusal to present God in this venturesome drama, in the spirited aloofness of his idea of Junius, proudly maintaining the opinions of his earthly life, and pre-eminently in the quiet, sympathetic beauty of his description of Saint Michael:

> Michael flew forth in glory and in good;
> A goodly work of Him from whom all glory
> And good arise...who wore
> The aspect of a god, but this ne'er nursed
> Pride in his heavenly bosom, in whose core
> No thought, save for his Maker's service, durst
> Intrude.

Byron's careless rhyme and construction were no hindrance to the more slipshod craftsmanship permissible in satire, and his epigrams no more lacked point than his strokes did weight, while his terseness admirably illustrates his view that

> Digression is a sin which to my mind
> Becomes exceeding tedious (*Beppo*).

Intensely sensitive to material matters, Byron seldom left the things of earth, but did more than Wordsworth himself to exemplify the latter's dictum that the language of everyday life can be made the language of poetry:

> Let's skip a few short years of hollow peace
> Which peopled earth no better, hell as wont
> And heaven none.

Probably, however, the greatest charm of *The Vision of Judgment* lies in the variety of its moods, ranging from the flippant picture of the Recording Angel, destitute of wing feathers which had all been used for quills, and hectically thinking out fresh remarks, to that of Saint Peter sneering at the parvenu Saint Paul, or the culminating irreverence of

> God save the King! It is a large economy
> In God to save the like.

Sometimes the wit of the author is grim, and there is ironical pathos in Satan's comment on the lymphatic king whose funeral had been a mockery of pomp and corruption, that "heaven could not make him better nor hell worse," so much more evil was the curse within him. Indeed, had the fates decreed for Byron a different life, there might have been added to his passionate arraignment a deeper pity and instead of seeking in reckless raillery a refuge for his irritated susceptibilities, he might have experienced a hopeful charity which his tortured nature never knew, while his toleration and acumen widened out into generosity and vision:

> God help me too! I am, God knows,
> As helpless as the devil can wish.

In these days, when levity more often greets orthodoxy than does acceptance, it is almost impossible to appreciate the courage which Byron required to write his *Vision*, but a closer study of his personality and of his times than can be attempted here reveals a nature that vibrated in opposition to pretence, and only failed to be constructive because it weakened defiance with remorse, and had not learnt that man only acquires liberty when he submits his soul willingly to imperial behests.

MARY LE H. REDMAN.

September 1926.

THE VISION OF JUDGMENT

BY

QUEVEDO REDIVIVUS

Suggested by the composition so entitled
by the author of "Wat Tyler"

"A Daniel come to judgment! yea, a Daniel!
I thank thee, Jew, for teaching me that word."

PREFACE

It hath been wisely said, that "One fool makes many"; and it hath been poetically observed—

"That fools rush in where angels fear to tread."

POPE.

If Mr Southey had not rushed in where he had no business, and where he never was before, and never will be again, the following poem would not have been written. It is not impossible that it may be as good as his own, seeing that it cannot, by any species of stupidity, natural or acquired, be *worse*. The gross flattery, the dull impudence, the renegado intolerance, and impious cant, of the poem by the author of "Wat Tyler," are something so stupendous as to form the sublime of himself—containing the quintessence of his own attributes.

So much for his poem—a word on his preface. In this preface it has pleased the magnanimous Laureate to draw the picture of a supposed "Satanic School," the which he doth recommend to the notice of the legislature; thereby adding to his other laurels the ambition of those of an informer. If there exists anywhere, except in his imagination, such a School, is he not sufficiently armed against it by his own intense vanity? The truth is, that there are certain writers whom Mr S. imagines, like Scrub, to have "talked of *him*; for they laughed consumedly."

I think I know enough of most of the writers to whom he is supposed to allude, to assert, that they, in their individual capacities, have done more good, in the charities of life, to their fellow-creatures, in any one year, than Mr Southey has done harm to himself by his absurdities in his whole life; and this is saying a great deal. But I have a few questions to ask.

1stly, Is Mr Southey the author of "Wat Tyler"?

2ndly, Was he not refused a remedy at law by the highest judge of his beloved England, because it was a blasphemous and seditious publication?

3rdly, Was he not entitled by William Smith, in full parliament, "a rancorous renegado"?

4thly, Is he not poet laureate, with his own lines on Martin the regicide staring him in the face?

And, 5thly, Putting the four preceding items together, with what conscience dare *he* call the attention of the laws to the publications of others, be they what they may?

I say nothing of the cowardice of such a proceeding, its meanness speaks for itself; but I wish to touch upon the *motive*, which is neither more nor less than that Mr S. has been laughed at a little in some recent publications, as he was of yore in the "Anti-Jacobin," by his present patrons. Hence all this "skimble-scamble stuff" about "Satanic," and so forth. However, it is worthy of him—"*qualis ab incepto.*"

If there is anything obnoxious to the political opinions of a portion of the public in the following poem, they may thank Mr Southey. He might have written hexameters, as he has written everything else, for aught that the writer cared—had they been upon another subject. But to attempt to canonise a monarch, who, whatever were his household virtues, was neither a successful nor a patriot king,—inasmuch as several years of his reign passed in war with America and Ireland, to say nothing of the aggression upon France, —like all other exaggeration, necessarily begets opposition. In whatever manner he may be spoken of in this new "Vision," his *public* career will not be more favourably transmitted by history. Of his private virtues (although a little expensive to the nation) there can be no doubt.

With regard to the supernatural personages treated of, I can only say that I know as much about them, and (as an honest man) have a better right to talk of them than Robert Southey. I have also treated them more tolerantly. The way in which that poor insane creature, the Laureate, deals about his judgments in the next world, is like his own judgment in this. If it was not completely ludicrous, it would be something worse. I don't think that there is much more to say at present.

QUEVEDO REDIVIVUS.

P.S.—It is possible that some readers may object, in these objectionable times, to the freedom with which saints, angels, and spiritual persons discourse in this "Vision." But, for precedents upon such points, I must refer him to Fielding's "Journey from this World to the next," and to the Visions of myself, the said Quevedo, in Spanish or translated. The reader is also requested to observe, that no doctrinal tenets are insisted upon or discussed; that the person of the Deity is carefully withheld from sight, which is more than can be said for the Laureate, who hath thought proper to make him talk, not "like a school-divine," but like the unscholarlike Mr Southey. The whole action passes on the outside of heaven; and Chaucer's "Wife of Bath," Pulci's "Morgante Maggiore," Swift's "Tale of a Tub," and the other works above referred to, are cases in point of the freedom with which saints, &c. may be permitted to converse in works not intended to be serious.

Q. R.

₊ Mr Southey being, as he says, a good Christian and vindictive, threatens, I understand, a reply to this our answer. It is to be hoped that his visionary faculties will in the mean time have acquired a little more judgment, properly so called: otherwise he will get himself into new dilemmas. These apostate Jacobins furnish rich rejoinders. Let him take a specimen. Mr Southey laudeth grievously "one Mr Landor," who cultivates much private renown in the shape of Latin verses; and not long ago, the poet laureate dedicated to him, it appeareth, one of his fugitive lyrics, upon the strength of a poem called "Gebir." Who could suppose, that in this same Gebir the aforesaid Savage Landor (for such is his grim cognomen)

putteth into the infernal regions no less a person than the hero of his friend Mr Southey's heaven,—yea, even George the Third! See also how personal Savage becometh, when he hath a mind. The following is his portrait of our late gracious sovereign:

(Prince Gebir having descended into the infernal regions, the shades of his royal ancestors are, at his request, called up to his view; and he exclaims to his ghostly guide)—

"Aroar, what wretch that nearest us? what wretch
Is that with eyebrows white and slanting brow?
Listen! him yonder who, bound down supine,
Shrinks yelling from that sword there, engine-hung.
He too amongst my ancestors! I hate
The despot, but the dastard I despise.
Was he our countryman?"
                              "Alas, O king!
Iberia bore him, but the breed accurst
Inclement winds blew blighting from north-east."
"He was a warrior then, nor fear'd the gods?"
"Gebir, he fear'd the demons, not the gods,
Though them indeed his daily face adored;
And was no warrior, yet the thousand lives
Squander'd, as stones to exercise a sling,
And the tame cruelty and cold caprice—
Oh madness of mankind! address'd, adored!"
                              Gebir, p. 28.

I omit noticing some edifying Ithyphallics of Savagius, wishing to keep the proper veil over them, if his grave but somewhat indiscreet worshipper will suffer it; but certainly these teachers of "great moral lessons" are apt to be found in strange company.

THE VISION OF JUDGMENT

I

SAINT PETER sat by the celestial gate:
  His keys were rusty, and the lock was dull,
So little trouble had been given of late;
  Not that the place by any means was full,
But since the Gallic era "eighty-eight"
  The devils had ta'en a longer, stronger pull,
And "a pull altogether," as they say
At sea—which drew most souls another way.

II

The angels all were singing out of tune,
  And hoarse with having little else to do,
Excepting to wind up the sun and moon,
  Or curb a runaway young star or two,
Or wild colt of a comet, which too soon
  Broke out of bounds o'er th'ethereal blue,
Splitting some planet with its playful tail,
As boats are sometimes by a wanton whale.

III

The guardian seraphs had retired on high,
  Finding their charges past all care below;
Terrestrial business fill'd nought in the sky
  Save the recording angel's black bureau;

Who found, indeed, the facts to multiply
  With such rapidity of vice and woe,
That he had stripp'd off both his wings in quills,
And yet was in arrear of human ills.

IV

His business so augmented of late years,
  That he was forced, against his will no doubt,
(Just like those cherubs, earthly ministers,)
  For some resource to turn himself about,
And claim the help of his celestial peers,
  To aid him ere he should be quite worn out
By the increased demand for his remarks:
Six angels and twelve saints were named his clerks.

V

This was a handsome board—at least for heaven;
  And yet they had even then enough to do,
So many conquerors' cars were daily driven,
  So many kingdoms fitted up anew;
Each day too slew its thousands six or seven,
  Till at the crowning carnage, Waterloo,
They threw their pens down in divine disgust—
The page was so besmear'd with blood and dust.

VI

This by the way; 'tis not mine to record
  What angels shrink from: even the very devil
On this occasion his own work abhorr'd,
  So surfeited with the infernal revel:
Though he himself had sharpen'd every sword,
  It almost quench'd his innate thirst of evil.
(Here Satan's sole good work deserves insertion—
'Tis, that he has both generals in reversion.)

VII

Let's skip a few short years of hollow peace,
  Which peopled earth no better, hell as wont,
And heaven none—they form the tyrant's lease,
  With nothing but new names subscribed upon't;
'Twill one day finish: meantime they increase,
  "With seven heads and ten horns," and all in front,
Like Saint John's foretold beast; but ours are born
Less formidable in the head than horn.

VIII

In the first year of freedom's second dawn
  Died George the Third; although no tyrant, one
Who shielded tyrants, till each sense withdrawn
  Left him nor mental nor external sun:

A better farmer ne'er brush'd dew from lawn,
　A worse king never left a realm undone!
He died—but left his subjects still behind,
One half as mad—and t'other no less blind.

IX

He died! his death made no great stir on earth:
　His burial made some pomp; there was profusion
Of velvet, gilding, brass, and no great dearth
　Of aught but tears—save those shed by collusion.
For these things may be bought at their true worth;
　Of elegy there was the due infusion—
Bought also; and the torches, cloaks, and banners,
Heralds, and relics of old Gothic manners,

X

Form'd a sepulchral melodrame. Of all
　The fools who flock'd to swell or see the show,
Who cared about the corpse? The funeral
　Made the attraction, and the black the woe.
There throbb'd not there a thought which pierced the
　　pall;
　And when the gorgeous coffin was laid low,
It seem'd the mockery of hell to fold
The rottenness of eighty years in gold.

XI

So mix his body with the dust! It might
   Return to what it *must* far sooner, were
The natural compound left alone to fight
   Its way back into earth, and fire, and air;
But the unnatural balsams merely blight
   What nature made him at his birth, as bare
As the mere million's base unmummied clay—
Yet all his spices but prolong decay.

XII

He's dead—and upper earth with him has done;
   He's buried; save the undertaker's bill,
Or lapidary scrawl, the world is gone
   For him, unless he left a German will:
But where's the proctor who will ask his son?
   In whom his qualities are reigning still,
Except that household virtue, most uncommon,
Of constancy to a bad, ugly woman.

XIII

"God save the king!" It is a large economy
   In God to save the like; but if he will
Be saving, all the better; for not one am I
   Of those who think damnation better still:

I hardly know too if not quite alone am I
   In this small hope of bettering future ill
By circumscribing, with some slight restriction,
The eternity of hell's hot jurisdiction.

XIV

I know this is unpopular; I know
   'Tis blasphemous; I know one may be damn'd
For hoping no one else may e'er be so;
   I know my catechism; I know we're cramm'd
With the best doctrines till we quite o'erflow;
   I know that all save England's church have shamm'd,
And that the other twice two hundred churches
And synagogues have made a *damn'd* bad purchase.

XV

God help us all! God help me too! I am,
   God knows, as helpless as the devil can wish,
And not a whit more difficult to damn,
   Than is to bring to land a late-hook'd fish,
Or to the butcher to purvey the lamb;
   Not that I'm fit for such a noble dish,
As one day will be that immortal fry
Of almost everybody born to die.

XVI

Saint Peter sat by the celestial gate,
    And nodded o'er his keys; when, lo! there came
A wondrous noise he had not heard of late—
    A rushing sound of wind, and stream, and flame;
In short, a roar of things extremely great,
    Which would have made aught save a saint exclaim;
But he, with first a start and then a wink,
Said, "There's another star gone out, I think!"

XVII

But ere he could return to his repose,
    A cherub flapp'd his right wing o'er his eyes—
At which St Peter yawn'd, and rubb'd his nose:
    "Saint porter," said the angel, "prithee rise!"
Waving a goodly wing, which glow'd, as glows
    An earthly peacock's tail, with heavenly dyes:
To which the saint replied, "Well, what's the matter?
Is Lucifer come back with all this clatter?"

XVIII

"No," quoth the cherub; "George the Third is dead."
    "And who *is* George the Third?" replied the
      apostle:
"*What George? what Third?*" "The king of England,"
      said
    The angel. "Well! he won't find kings to jostle

Him on his way; but does he wear his head?
  Because the last we saw here had a tussle,
And ne'er would have got into heaven's good graces,
Had he not flung his head in all our faces.

XIX

"He was, if I remember, king of France;
  That head of his, which could not keep a crown
On earth, yet ventured in my face to advance
  A claim to those of martyrs—like my own:
If I had had my sword, as I had once
  When I cut ears off, I had cut him down;
But having but my *keys*, and not my brand,
I only knock'd his head from out his hand.

XX

"And then he set up such a headless howl,
  That all the saints came out and took him in;
And there he sits by St Paul, cheek by jowl;
  That fellow Paul—the parvenù! The skin
Of St Bartholomew, which makes his cowl
  In heaven, and upon earth redeem'd his sin,
So as to make a martyr, never sped
Better than did this weak and wooden head.

XXI

"But had it come up here upon its shoulders,
  There would have been a different tale to tell:
The fellow-feeling in the saint's beholders
  Seems to have acted on them like a spell,
And so this very foolish head heaven solders
  Back on its trunk: it may be very well,
And seems the custom here to overthrow
Whatever has been wisely done below."

XXII

The angel answer'd, "Peter! do not pout:
  The king who comes has head and all entire,
And never knew much what it was about—
  He did as doth the puppet—by its wire,
And will be judged like all the rest, no doubt:
  My business and your own is not to inquire
Into such matters, but to mind our cue—
Which is to act as we are bid to do."

XXIII

While thus they spake, the angelic caravan,
  Arriving like a rush of mighty wind,
Cleaving the fields of space, as doth the swan
  Some silver stream (say Ganges, Nile, or Inde,

Or Thames, or Tweed), and 'midst them an old man
   With an old soul, and both extremely blind,
Halted before the gate, and in his shroud
Seated their fellow-traveller on a cloud.

XXIV

But bringing up the rear of this bright host
   A Spirit of a different aspect waved
His wings, like thunder-clouds above some coast
   Whose barren beach with frequent wrecks is paved;
His brow was like the deep when tempest-toss'd;
   Fierce and unfathomable thoughts engraved
Eternal wrath on his immortal face,
And *where* he gazed a gloom pervaded space.

XXV

As he drew near, he gazed upon the gate
   Ne'er to be enter'd more by him or Sin,
With such a glance of supernatural hate,
   As made Saint Peter wish himself within;
He patter'd with his keys at a great rate,
   And sweated through his apostolic skin:
Of course his perspiration was but ichor,
Or some such other spiritual liquor.

XXVI

The very cherubs huddled all together,
  Like birds when soars the falcon; and they felt
A tingling to the tip of every feather,
  And form'd a circle like Orion's belt
Around their poor old charge; who scarce knew whither
  His guards had led him, though they gently dealt
With royal manes (for by many stories,
And true, we learn the angels all are Tories).

XXVII

As things were in this posture, the gate flew
  Asunder, and the flashing of its hinges
Flung over space an universal hue
  Of many-colour'd flame, until its tinges
Reach'd even our speck of earth, and made a new
  Aurora borealis spread its fringes
O'er the North Pole; the same seen, when ice-bound,
By Captain Parry's crew, in "Melville's Sound."

XXVIII

And from the gate thrown open issued beaming
  A beautiful and mighty Thing of Light,
Radiant with glory, like a banner streaming
  Victorious from some world-o'erthrowing fight:

My poor comparisons must needs be teeming
  With earthly likenesses, for here the night
Of clay obscures our best conceptions, saving
  Johanna Southcote, or Bob Southey raving.

XXIX

'Twas the archangel Michael; all men know
  The make of angels and archangels, since
There's scarce a scribbler has not one to show,
  From the fiends' leader to the angels' prince;
There also are some altar-pieces, though
  I really can't say that they much evince
One's inner notions of immortal spirits;
But let the connoisseurs explain *their* merits.

XXX

Michael flew forth in glory and in good;
  A goodly work of him from whom all glory
And good arise; the portal past—he stood;
  Before him the young cherubs and saints hoary—
(I say *young*, begging to be understood
  By looks, not years; and should be very sorry
To state, they were not older than St Peter,
But merely that they seem'd a little sweeter).

R B   2

XXXI

The cherubs and the saints bow'd down before
  That arch-angelic hierarch, the first
Of essences angelical, who wore
  The aspect of a god; but this ne'er nursed
Pride in his heavenly bosom, in whose core
  No thought, save for his Maker's service, durst
Intrude, however glorified and high;
He knew him but the viceroy of the sky.

XXXII

He and the sombre, silent Spirit met—
  They knew each other both for good and ill;
Such was their power, that neither could forget
  His former friend and future foe; but still
There was a high, immortal, proud regret
  In either's eye, as if 'twere less their will
Than destiny to make the eternal years
Their date of war, and their "champ clos" the spheres.

XXXIII

But here they were in neutral space: we know
  From Job, that Satan hath the power to pay
A heavenly visit thrice a year or so;
  And that the "sons of God," like those of clay,

Must keep him company; and we might show
   From the same book, in how polite a way
The dialogue is held between the Powers
Of Good and Evil—but 'twould take up hours.

XXXIV

And this is not a theologic tract,
   To prove with Hebrew and with Arabic,
If Job be allegory or a fact,
   But a true narrative; and thus I pick
From out the whole but such and such an act
   As sets aside the slightest thought of trick.
'Tis every tittle true, beyond suspicion,
And accurate as any other vision.

XXXV

The spirits were in neutral space, before
   The gate of heaven; like eastern thresholds is
The place where Death's grand cause is argued o'er,
   And souls despatch'd to that world or to this;
And therefore Michael and the other wore
   A civil aspect: though they did not kiss,
Yet still between his Darkness and his Brightness
There pass'd a mutual glance of great politeness.

XXXVI

The Archangel bow'd, not like a modern beau,
But with a graceful Oriental bend,
Pressing one radiant arm just where below
The heart in good men is supposed to tend;
He turn'd as to an equal, not too low,
But kindly; Satan met his ancient friend
With more hauteur, as might an old Castilian
Poor noble meet a mushroom rich civilian.

XXXVII

He merely bent his diabolic brow
An instant; and then raising it, he stood
In act to assert his right or wrong, and show
Cause why King George by no means could or
should
Make out a case to be exempt from woe
Eternal, more than other kings, endued
With better sense and hearts, whom history mentions,
Who long have "paved hell with their good inten-
tions."

XXXVIII

Michael began: "What wouldst thou with this man,
Now dead, and brought before the Lord? What ill
Hath he wrought since his mortal race began,
That thou canst claim him? Speak! and do thy will,

If it be just: if in this earthly span
  He hath been greatly failing to fulfil
His duties as a king and mortal, say,
And he is thine; if not, let him have way."

XXXIX

"Michael!" replied the Prince of Air, "even here,
  Before the Gate of him thou servest, must
I claim my subject: and will make appear
  That as he was my worshipper in dust,
So shall he be in spirit, although dear
  To thee and thine, because nor wine nor lust
Were of his weaknesses; yet on the throne
He reign'd o'er millions to serve me alone.

XL

"Look to *our* earth, or rather *mine*; it was,
  Once, *more* thy master's: but I triumph not
In this poor planet's conquest; nor, alas!
  Need he thou servest envy me my lot:
With all the myriads of bright worlds which pass
  In worship round him, he may have forgot
Yon weak creation of such paltry things:
I think few worth damnation save their kings,—

XLI

"And these but as a kind of quit-rent, to
   Assert my right as lord: and even had
I such an inclination, 'twere (as you
   Well know) superfluous; they are grown so bad,
That hell has nothing better left to do
   Than leave them to themselves: so much more mad
And evil by their own internal curse,
Heaven cannot make them better, nor I worse.

XLII

"Look to the earth, I said, and say again:
   When this old, blind, mad, helpless, weak, poor
     worm
Began in youth's first bloom and flush to reign,
   The world and he both wore a different form,
And much of earth and all the watery plain
   Of ocean call'd him king: through many a storm
His isles had floated on the abyss of time;
For the rough virtues chose them for their clime.

XLIII

"He came to his sceptre young; he leaves it old:
   Look to the state in which he found his realm,
And left it; and his annals too behold,
   How to a minion first he gave the helm;

How grew upon his heart a thirst for gold,
  The beggar's vice, which can but overwhelm
The meanest hearts; and for the rest, but glance
Thine eye along America and France.

XLIV

" 'Tis true, he was a tool from first to last
  (I have the workmen safe); but as a tool
So let him be consumed. From out the past
  Of ages, since mankind have known the rule
Of monarchs—from the bloody rolls amass'd
  Of sin and slaughter—from the Cæsar's school,
Take the worst pupil; and produce a reign
More drench'd with gore, more cumber'd with the
      slain.

XLV

" He ever warr'd with freedom and the free:
  Nations as men, home subjects, foreign foes,
So that they utter'd the word ' Liberty!'
  Found George the Third their first opponent.Whose
History was ever stain'd as his will be
  With national and individual woes?
I grant his household abstinence; I grant
His neutral virtues, which most monarchs want;

XLVI

" I know he was a constant consort; own
   He was a decent sire, and middling lord.
All this is much, and most upon a throne;
   As temperance, if at Apicius' board,
Is more than at an anchorite's supper shown.
   I grant him all the kindest can accord;
And this was well for him, but not for those
Millions who found him what oppression chose.

XLVII

" The New World shook him off; the Old yet groans
   Beneath what he and his prepared, if not
Completed: he leaves heirs on many thrones
   To all his vices, without what begot
Compassion for him—his tame virtues; drones
   Who sleep, or despots who have now forgot
A lesson which shall be re-taught them, wake
Upon the thrones of earth; but let them quake!

XLVIII

" Five millions of the primitive, who hold
   The faith which makes ye great on earth, implored
A *part* of that vast *all* they held of old,—
   Freedom to worship—not alone your Lord,

Michael, but you, and you, Saint Peter! Cold
  Must be your souls, if you have not abhorr'd
The foe to Catholic participation
In all the license of a Christian nation.

XLIX

"True! he allow'd them to pray God; but as
  A consequence of prayer, refused the law
Which would have placed them upon the same base
  With those who did not hold the saints in awe."
But here Saint Peter started from his place,
  And cried, "You may the prisoner withdraw:
Ere heaven shall ope her portals to this Guelph,
While I am guard, may I be damn'd myself!

L

"Sooner will I with Cerberus exchange
  My office (and *his* is no sinecure)
Than see this royal Bedlam bigot range
  The azure fields of heaven, of that be sure!"
"Saint!" replied Satan, "you do well to avenge
  The wrongs he made your satellites endure;
And if to this exchange you should be given,
I'll try to coax *our* Cerberus up to heaven!"

LI

Here Michael interposed: "Good saint! and devil!
   Pray, not so fast; you both outrun discretion.
Saint Peter! you were wont to be more civil!
   Satan! excuse this warmth of his expression,
And condescension to the vulgar's level:
   Even saints sometimes forget themselves in session.
Have you got more to say?"—"No."—"If you please,
I'll trouble you to call your witnesses."

LII

Then Satan turn'd and waved his swarthy hand,
   Which stirr'd with its electric qualities
Clouds farther off than we can understand,
   Although we find him sometimes in our skies;
Infernal thunder shook both sea and land
   In all the planets, and hell's batteries
Let off the artillery, which Milton mentions
As one of Satan's most sublime inventions.

LIII

This was a signal unto such damn'd souls
   As have the privilege of their damnation
Extended far beyond the mere controls
   Of worlds past, present, or to come; no station

Is theirs particularly in the rolls
  Of hell assign'd; but where their inclination
Or business carries them in search of game,
They may range freely—being damn'd the same.

LIV

They're proud of this—as very well they may,
  It being a sort of knighthood, or gilt key
Stuck in their loins; or like to an "entré"
  Up the back stairs, or such free-masonry.
I borrow my comparisons from clay,
  Being clay myself. Let not those spirits be
Offended with such base low likenesses;
We know their posts are nobler far than these.

LV

When the great signal ran from heaven to hell—
  About ten million times the distance reckon'd
From our sun to its earth, as we can tell
  How much time it takes up, even to a second,
For every ray that travels to dispel
  The fogs of London, through which, dimly beacon'd,
The weathercocks are gilt some thrice a year,
If that the *summer* is not too severe:

LVI

I say that I can tell—'twas half a minute;
  I know the solar beams take up more time
Ere, pack'd up for their journey, they begin it;
  But then their telegraph is less sublime,
And if they ran a race, they would not win it
  'Gainst Satan's couriers bound for their own clime.
The sun takes up some years for every ray
To reach its goal—the devil not half a day.

LVII

Upon the verge of space, about the size
  Of half-a-crown, a little speck appear'd
(I've seen a something like it in the skies
  In the Ægean, ere a squall); it near'd,
And, growing bigger, took another guise;
  Like an aërial ship it tack'd, and steer'd,
Or *was* steer'd (I am doubtful of the grammar
Of the last phrase, which makes the stanza stammer;—

LVIII

But take your choice): and then it grew a cloud;
  And so it was—a cloud of witnesses.
But such a cloud! No land e'er saw a crowd
  Of locusts numerous as the heavens saw these;

They shadow'd with their myriads space; their loud
 And varied cries were like those of wild geese
(If nations may be liken'd to a goose),
And realised the phrase of "hell broke loose."

LIX

Here crash'd a sturdy oath of stout John Bull,
 Who damn'd away his eyes as heretofore:
There Paddy brogued "By Jasus!"—"What's your
  wull?"
  The temperate Scot exclaim'd: the French ghost
  swore
In certain terms I shan't translate in full,
 As the first coachman will; and 'midst the war,
The voice of Jonathan was heard to express,
"*Our* president is going to war, I guess."

LX

Besides there were the Spaniard, Dutch, and Dane;
 In short, an universal shoal of shades,
From Otaheite's isle to Salisbury Plain,
 Of all climes and professions, years and trades,
Ready to swear against the good king's reign,
 Bitter as clubs in cards are against spades:
All summon'd by this grand " subpœna," to
Try if kings mayn't be damn'd like me or you.

LXI

When Michael saw this host, he first grew pale,
 As angels can; next, like Italian twilight,
He turn'd all colours—as a peacock's tail,
 Or sunset streaming through a Gothic skylight
In some old abbey, or a trout not stale,
 Or distant lightning on the horizon *by* night,
Or a fresh rainbow, or a grand review
Of thirty regiments in red, green, and blue.

LXII

Then he address'd himself to Satan: "Why—
 My good old friend, for such I deem you, though
Our different parties make us fight so shy,
 I ne'er mistake you for a *personal* foe;
Our difference is *political*, and I
 Trust that, whatever may occur below,
You know my great respect for you: and this
Makes me regret whate'er you do amiss—

LXIII

"Why, my dear Lucifer, would you abuse
 My call for witnesses? I did not mean
That you should half of earth and hell produce;
 'Tis even superfluous, since two honest, clean,

True testimonies are enough: we lose
   Our time, nay, our eternity, between
The accusation and defence: if we
Hear both, 'twill stretch our immortality."

LXIV

Satan replied, "To me the matter is
   Indifferent, in a personal point of view:
I can have fifty better souls than this
   With far less trouble than we have gone through
Already; and I merely argued his
   Late majesty of Britain's case with you
Upon a point of form: you may dispose
Of him; I've kings enough below, God knows!"

LXV

Thus spoke the Demon (late call'd "multifaced"
   By multo-scribbling Southey). "Then we'll call
One or two persons of the myriads placed
   Around our congress, and dispense with all
The rest," quoth Michael: "Who may be so graced
   As to speak first? there's choice enough—who shall
It be?" Then Satan answer'd, "There are many;
But you may choose Jack Wilkes as well as any."

LXVI

A merry, cock-eyed, curious-looking sprite
  Upon the instant started from the throng,
Dress'd in a fashion now forgotten quite;
  For all the fashions of the flesh stick long
By people in the next world; where unite
  All the costumes since Adam's, right or wrong,
From Eve's fig-leaf down to the petticoat,
Almost as scanty, of days less remote.

LXVII

The spirit look'd around upon the crowds
  Assembled, and exclaim'd, "My friends of all
The spheres, we shall catch cold amongst these clouds;
  So let's to business: why this general call?
If those are freeholders I see in shrouds,
  And 'tis for an election that they bawl,
Behold a candidate with unturn'd coat!
Saint Peter, may I count upon your vote?"

LXVIII

"Sir," replied Michael, "you mistake; these things
  Are of a former life, and what we do
Above is more august; to judge of kings
  Is the tribunal met: so now you know."

"Then I presume those gentlemen with wings,"
  Said Wilkes, "are cherubs; and that soul below
Looks much like George the Third, but to my mind
A good deal older—Bless me! is he blind?"

LXIX

"He is what you behold him, and his doom
  Depends upon his deeds," the Angel said;
"If you have aught to arraign in him, the tomb
  Gives license to the humblest beggar's head
To lift itself against the loftiest."—"Some,"
  Said Wilkes, "don't wait to see them laid in lead,
For such a liberty—and I, for one,
Have told them what I thought beneath the sun."

LXX

"*Above* the sun repeat, then, what thou hast
  To urge against him," said the Archangel. "Why,"
Replied the spirit, "since old scores are past,
  Must I turn evidence? In faith, not I.
Besides, I beat him hollow at the last,
  With all his Lords and Commons: in the sky
I don't like ripping up old stories, since
His conduct was but natural in a prince.

LXXI

"Foolish, no doubt, and wicked, to oppress
   A poor unlucky devil without a shilling;
But then I blame the man himself much less
   Than Bute and Grafton, and shall be unwilling
To see him punish'd here for their excess,
   Since they were both damn'd long ago, and still in
Their place below: for me, I have forgiven,
And vote his 'habeas corpus' into heaven."

LXXII

"Wilkes," said the Devil, "I understand all this;
   You turn'd to half a courtier ere you died,
And seem to think it would not be amiss
   To grow a whole one on the other side
Of Charon's ferry; you forget that *his*
   Reign is concluded; whatsoe'er betide,
He won't be sovereign more: you've lost your labour,
For at the best he will but be your neighbour.

LXXIII

"However, I knew what to think of it,
   When I beheld you in your jesting way,
Flitting and whispering round about the spit
   Where Belial, upon duty for the day,

With Fox's lard was basting William Pitt,
   His pupil; I knew what to think, I say:
That fellow even in hell breeds farther ills;
I'll have him *gagg'd*—'twas one of his own bills.

LXXIV

"Call Junius!" From the crowd a shadow stalk'd,
   And at the name there was a general squeeze,
So that the very ghosts no longer walk'd
   In comfort, at their own aërial ease,
But were all ramm'd, and jamm'd (but to be balk'd,
   As we shall see), and jostled hands and knees,
Like wind compress'd and pent within a bladder,
Or like a human colic, which is sadder.

LXXV

The shadow came—a tall, thin, grey-hair'd figure,
   That look'd as it had been a shade on earth;
Quick in its motions, with an air of vigour,
   But nought to mark its breeding or its birth;
Now it wax'd little, then again grew bigger,
   With now an air of gloom, or savage mirth;
But as you gazed upon its features, they
Changed every instant—to *what*, none could say.

LXXVI

The more intently the ghosts gazed, the less
   Could they distinguish whose the features were;
The Devil himself seem'd puzzled even to guess;
   They varied like a dream—now here, now there;
And several people swore from out the press,
   They knew him perfectly; and one could swear
He was his father: upon which another
Was sure he was his mother's cousin's brother:

LXXVII

Another, that he was a duke, or knight,
   An orator, a lawyer, or a priest,
A nabob, a man-midwife; but the wight
   Mysterious changed his countenance at least
As oft as they their minds; though in full sight
   He stood, the puzzle only was increased;
The man was a phantasmagoria in
Himself—he was so volatile and thin.

LXXVIII

The moment that you had pronounced him *one*,
   Presto! his face changed, and he was another;
And when that change was hardly well put on,
   It varied, till I don't think his own mother

(If that he had a mother) would her son
 Have known, he shifted so from one to t'other;
Till guessing from a pleasure grew a task,
At this epistolary "Iron Mask."

LXXIX

For sometimes he like Cerberus would seem—
 "Three gentlemen at once" (as sagely says
Good Mrs Malaprop); then you might deem
 That he was not even *one*; now many rays
Were flashing round him; and now a thick steam
 Hid him from sight—like fogs on London days:
Now Burke, now Tooke, he grew to people's fancies,
And certes often like Sir Philip Francis.

LXXX

I've an hypothesis—'tis quite my own;
 I never let it out till now, for fear
Of doing people harm about the throne,
 And injuring some minister or peer,
On whom the stigma might perhaps be blown;
 It is—my gentle public, lend thine ear!
'Tis, that what Junius we are wont to call
Was *really*, *truly*, nobody at all.

LXXXI

I don't see wherefore letters should not be
    Written without hands, since we daily view
Them written without heads; and books, we see,
    Are fill'd as well without the latter too:
And really till we fix on somebody
    For certain sure to claim them as his due,
Their author, like the Niger's mouth, will bother
The world to say if *there* be mouth or author.

LXXXII

"And who and what art thou?" the Archangel said.
    "For *that* you may consult my title-page,"
Replied this mighty shadow of a shade:
    "If I have kept my secret half an age,
I scarce shall tell it now."—"Canst thou upbraid,"
    Continued Michael, "George Rex, or allege
Aught further?" Junius answer'd, "You had better
First ask him for *his* answer to my letter:

LXXXIII

"My charges upon record will outlast
    The brass of both his epitaph and tomb."
"Repent'st thou not," said Michael, "of some past
    Exaggeration? something which may doom

Thyself if false, as him if true? Thou wast
   Too bitter—is it not so?—in thy gloom
Of passion?"—"Passion!" cried the phantom dim,
"I loved my country, and I hated him.

LXXXIV

"What I have written, I have written: let
   The rest be on his head or mine!" So spoke
Old "Nominis Umbra"; and while speaking yet,
   Away he melted in celestial smoke.
Then Satan said to Michael, "Don't forget
   To call George Washington, and John Horne Tooke,
And Franklin";—but at this time there was heard
A cry for room, though not a phantom stirr'd.

LXXXV

At length with jostling, elbowing, and the aid
   Of cherubim appointed to that post,
The devil Asmodeus to the circle made
   His way, and look'd as if his journey cost
Some trouble. When his burden down he laid,
   "What's this?" cried Michael; "why, 'tis not a
      ghost?"
"I know it," quoth the incubus; "but he
Shall be one, if you leave the affair to me.

LXXXVI

"Confound the renegado! I have sprain'd
  My left wing, he's so heavy; one would think
Some of his works about his neck were chain'd.
  But to the point; while hovering o'er the brink
Of Skiddaw (where as usual it still rain'd),
  I saw a taper, far below me, wink,
And stooping, caught this fellow at a libel—
No less on history than the Holy Bible.

LXXXVII

"The former is the devil's scripture, and
  The latter yours, good Michael: so the affair
Belongs to all of us, you understand.
  I snatch'd him up just as you see him there,
And brought him off for sentence out of hand:
  I've scarcely been ten minutes in the air—
At least a quarter it can hardly be:
I dare say that his wife is still at tea."

LXXXVIII

Here Satan said, "I know this man of old,
  And have expected him for some time here;
A sillier fellow you will scarce behold,
  Or more conceited in his petty sphere:

But surely it was not worth while to fold
    Such trash below your wing, Asmodeus dear:
We had the poor wretch safe (without being bored
With carriage) coming of his own accord.

LXXXIX

"But since he's here, let's see what he has done."
    "Done!" cried Asmodeus, "he anticipates
The very business you are now upon,
    And scribbles as if head clerk to the Fates.
Who knows to what his ribaldry may run,
    When such an ass as this, like Balaam's, prates?"
"Let's hear," quoth Michael, "what he has to say:
You know we're bound to that in every way."

XC

Now the bard, glad to get an audience, which
    By no means often was his case below,
Began to cough, and hawk, and hem, and pitch
    His voice into that awful note of woe
To all unhappy hearers within reach
    Of poets when the tide of rhyme's in flow;
But stuck fast with his first hexameter,
Not one of all whose gouty feet would stir.

XCI

But ere the spavin'd dactyls could be spurr'd
   Into recitative, in great dismay
Both cherubim and seraphim were heard
   To murmur loudly through their long array;
And Michael rose ere he could get a word
   Of all his founder'd verses under way,
And cried, "For God's sake stop, my friend! 'twere
    best—
Non Di, non homines—you know the rest."

XCII

A general bustle spread throughout the throng,
   Which seem'd to hold all verse in detestation;
The angels had of course enough of song
   When upon service; and the generation
Of ghosts had heard too much in life, not long
   Before, to profit by a new occasion:
The monarch, mute till then, exclaim'd, "What! what!
Pye come again? No more—no more of that!"

XCIII

The tumult grew; an universal cough
   Convulsed the skies, as during a debate,
When Castlereagh has been up long enough
   (Before he was first minister of state,

I mean—the *slaves hear now*); some cried "Off, off!"
   As at a farce; till, grown quite desperate,
The bard Saint Peter pray'd to interpose
(Himself an author) only for his prose.

XCIV

The varlet was not an ill-favour'd knave;
   A good deal like a vulture in the face,
With a hook nose and a hawk's eye, which gave
   A smart and sharper-looking sort of grace
To his whole aspect, which, though rather grave,
   Was by no means so ugly as his case;
But that, indeed, was hopeless as can be,
Quite a poetic felony "*de se*."

XCV

Then Michael blew his trump, and still'd the noise
   With one still greater, as is yet the mode
On earth besides; except some grumbling voice,
   Which now and then will make a slight inroad
Upon decorous silence, few will twice
   Lift up their lungs when fairly overcrow'd;
And now the bard could plead his own bad cause,
With all the attitudes of self-applause.

XCVI

He said—(I only give the heads)—he said,
  He meant no harm in scribbling; 'twas his way
Upon all topics; 'twas, besides, his bread,
  Of which he butter'd both sides; 'twould delay
Too long the assembly (he was pleased to dread),
  And take up rather more time than a day,
To name his works—he would but cite a few—
"Wat Tyler"—"Rhymes on Blenheim"—"Water-
    loo."

XCVII

He had written praises of a regicide;
  He had written praises of all kings whatever;
He had written for republics far and wide,
  And then against them bitterer than ever;
For pantisocracy he once had cried
  Aloud, a scheme less moral than 'twas clever;
Then grew a hearty anti-Jacobin—
Had turn'd his coat—and would have turn'd his skin.

XCVIII

He had sung against all battles, and again
  In their high praise and glory; he had call'd
Reviewing "the ungentle craft," and then
  Become as base a critic as e'er crawl'd—

Fed, paid, and pamper'd by the very men
  By whom his muse and morals had been maul'd:
He had written much blank verse, and blanker prose,
And more of both than anybody knows.

XCIX

He had written Wesley's life:—here turning round
  To Satan, "Sir, I'm ready to write yours,
In two octavo volumes, nicely bound,
  With notes and preface, all that most allures
The pious purchaser; and there's no ground
  For fear, for I can choose my own reviewers:
So let me have the proper documents,
That I may add you to my other saints."

C

Satan bow'd, and was silent. "Well, if you,
  With amiable modesty, decline
My offer, what says Michael? There are few
  Whose memoirs could be render'd more divine.
Mine is a pen of all work; not so new
  As it was once, but I would make you shine
Like your own trumpet. By the way, my own
Has more of brass in it, and is as well blown.

CI

"But talking about trumpets, here's my Vision!
   Now you shall judge, all people; yes, you shall
Judge with my judgment, and by my decision
   Be guided who shall enter heaven or fall.
I settle all these things by intuition,
   Times present, past, to come, heaven, hell, and all,
Like King Alfonso. When I thus see double,
I save the Deity some worlds of trouble."

CII

He ceased, and drew forth an MS.; and no
   Persuasion on the part of devils, saints,
Or angels, now could stop the torrent; so
   He read the first three lines of the contents;
But at the fourth, the whole spiritual show
   Had vanish'd, with variety of scents,
Ambrosial and sulphureous, as they sprang,
Like lightning, off from his "melodious twang."

CIII

Those grand heroics acted as a spell:
   The angels stopp'd their ears and plied their
      pinions;
The devils ran howling, deafen'd, down to hell;
   The ghosts fled, gibbering, for their own domin-
      ions—

(For 'tis not yet decided where they dwell,
 And I leave every man to his opinions);
Michael took refuge in his trump—but, lo!
His teeth were set on edge, he could not blow!

CIV

Saint Peter, who has hitherto been known
 For an impetuous saint, upraised his keys,
And at the fifth line knock'd the poet down;
 Who fell like Phæton, but more at ease,
Into his lake, for there he did not drown;
 A different web being by the Destinies
Woven for the Laureate's final wreath, whene'er
Reform shall happen either here or there.

CV

He first sank to the bottom—like his works,
 But soon rose to the surface—like himself;
For all corrupted things are buoy'd like corks,
 By their own rottenness, light as an elf,
Or wisp that flits o'er a morass: he lurks,
 It may be, still, like dull books on a shelf,
In his own den, to scrawl some "Life" or "Vision,"
As Welborn says—"the devil turn'd precisian."

CVI

As for the rest, to come to the conclusion
   Of this true dream, the telescope is gone
Which kept my optics free from all delusion,
   And show'd me what I in my turn have shown;
All I saw farther, in the last confusion,
   Was, that King George slipp'd into heaven for one;
And when the tumult dwindled to a calm,
I left him practising the hundredth psalm.

CAMBRIDGE PLAIN TEXTS   *Complete List:*

ENGLISH

Bacon. THE ADVANCEMENT OF LEARNING. Book I.
Carlyle. THE PRESENT TIME.
Donne. SERMONS XV AND LXVI.
Fuller. THE HOLY STATE (II, 1–15).
Goldsmith. THE GOOD-NATUR'D MAN.
Henryson. THE TESTAMENT OF CRESSEID.
Hooker. PREFACE TO "THE LAWS OF ECCLESIASTICAL POLITY."
Johnson. PAPERS FROM "THE IDLER."
Montaigne. FIVE ESSAYS, translated by John Florio.
Spenser. THE SHEPHEARDS CALENDAR.

FRENCH

Bossuet. ORAISONS FUNÈBRES.
De Musset. CARMOSINE.
Descartes. DISCOURS DE LA MÉTHODE.
Diderot. PARADOXE SUR LE COMÉDIEN.
Dumas. HISTOIRE DE MES BÊTES.
Gautier. MÉNAGERIE INTIME.
Hugo, Victor. EVIRADNUS, RATBERT (La Légende des Siècles).
La Bruyère. LES CARACTÈRES, OU LES MŒURS DE CE SIÈCLE.
Lamartine. MÉDITATIONS.
Michelet. SAINT-LOUIS.
Molière. L'AMOUR MÉDECIN. LE SICILIEN.
Molière. L'IMPROMPTU DE VERSAILLES.
Montalembert. DE L'AVENIR POLITIQUE DE L'ANGLETERRE.
Pascal. LETTRES ÉCRITES À UN PROVINCIAL.

GERMAN

Grillparzer. DER ARME SPIELMANN. ERINNERUNGEN AN BEET-
    HOVEN.
Herder. KLEINERE AUFSÄTZE I.
Hoffmann. DER KAMPF DER SÄNGER.
Lessing. HAMBURGISCHE DRAMATURGIE I.
Lessing. HAMBURGISCHE DRAMATURGIE II.

ITALIAN

Alfieri. LA VIRTÙ SCONOSCIUTA.
Gozzi, Gasparo. LA GAZZETTA VENETA.
Leopardi. PENSIERI.
Mazzini. FEDE E AVVENIRE.
Rosmini. CINQUE PIAGHE.

SPANISH

Simon Bolivar. ADDRESS TO THE VENEZUELAN CONGRESS AT
    ANGOSTURA, FEBRUARY 15, 1819.
Calderón. LA CENA DE BALTASAR.
Cervantes. PROLOGUES AND EPILOGUE.
Cervantes. RINCONETE Y CORTADILLO.
Espronceda. EL ESTUDIANTE DE SALAMANCA.
Luis de Leon. POESÍAS ORIGINALES.
Lope de Vega. EL MEJOR ALCALDE. EL REY.
Old Spanish Ballads.
Villegas. EL ABENCERRAJE.
Villena: Lebrija: Encina. SELECTIONS.

SOME PRESS OPINIONS

"These are delightful, slim little books....The print is very clear and pleasant to the eye....These Cambridge Plain Texts are just the kind of book that a lover of letters longs to put in his pocket as a prophylactic against boredom."—*The New Statesman*

"These little books...are exquisitely printed on excellent paper and are prefaced in each case by a brief biographical note concerning the author: otherwise entirely unencumbered with notes or explanatory matter, they form the most delicious and companionable little volumes we remember to have seen. The title-page is a model of refined taste—*simplex munditiis*."—*The Anglo-French Review*

"With their admirable print, the little books do credit to the great Press which is responsible for them."
Notes and Queries

"The series of texts of notable Italian works which is being issued at Cambridge should be made known wherever there is a chance of studying the language; they are clear, in a handy form, and carefully edited....The venture deserves well of all who aim at the higher culture."
The Inquirer

"Selections of this kind, made by competent hands, may serve to make us acquainted with much that we should otherwise miss. To read two of Donne's tremendous sermons may send many readers eagerly to enlarge their knowledge of one of the great glories of the English pulpit."—*The Holborn Review*

"This new Spanish text-book, printed on excellent paper, in delightfully clear type and of convenient pocket size, preserves the high level of achievement that characterises the series."—*The Teacher's World* on "Cervantes: Prologues and Epilogue"

"It is difficult to praise too highly the Cambridge Plain Texts."—*The London Mercury*

www.ingramcontent.com/pod-product-compliance
Ingram Content Group UK Ltd.
Pitfield, Milton Keynes, MK11 3LW, UK
UKHW042148280225
455719UK00001B/201